FAVOR
THE ROAD
TO SUCCESS

FAVOR
THE ROAD
TO SUCCESS

Bob Buess

Whitaker House

FAVOR, THE ROAD TO SUCCESS

Bob Buess
Sweeter Than Honey
P.O. Box 7110
Tyler, TX 75711

ISBN: 0-88368-251-6
Printed in the United States of America
Copyright © 1975 by Bob Buess

Whitaker House
30 Hunt Valley Circle
New Kensington, PA 15068

5 6 7 8 9 10 11 12 13 14 / 06 05 04 03 02 01 00 99 98

Introduction

This message has been in my spirit for about eight years. I have been ministering it to others with dramatic changes coming to pass in their lives as a result.

This message will have a powerful influence upon your life—if you will allow it to minister to your spirit.

Many people, due to childhood experiences, bad situations in marriage, or other reasons, withdraw into a shell of fear, frustration, or negativism.

This truth will help such a person release the Lord Jesus who is within him to a full, exciting, and exuberant life. This person will begin living with excitement, expecting to meet happy people.

Favor will begin to flow.

You will reap what you sow. Expect good things to happen, and that will be the things that start happening to you.

Thoughts are the beginning of reality.

The Holy Spirit plants good thoughts into your mind. As you meditate upon these positive thoughts, they are transferred to your spirit.

Once these thoughts are planted in the spirit, life begins to grow. Your life is controlled by the things which you place in your spirit by way of the thought pattern.

Sow negatives into your spirit, and you will constantly meet sour people. This spirit brings out the meanness in others.

Jesus increased in favor with God and man.

He had so much favor that he constantly had to tell people to "keep quiet" about their healings, etc.

He had so much favor that five thousand men plus women and children followed Him to a resort where He had planned a rest for Himself and His disciples.

He had so much favor that He nearly had to insult Pilate to get Himself crucified.

Favor teaching does not guarantee freedom from all problems and all persecutions. The religious leaders still demanded that Jesus be crucified.

Enjoy these strong positive teachings on

favor, but maintain a balance. There is another side to everything.

You will always find some who will not like you, but you must never allow this spirit to operate within you. You must continue to be forgiving and kind.

There have been many reconciliations between husband and wife after applying the truth of this message.

Others have found job opportunities which would have been lost to them.

Pass this book on to others.

Chapter 1

FAVOR CHANGES INSECURITY INTO SELF CONFIDENCE

Nobody liked her. She didn't even like herself. She was good looking, but she could not even get a date with a boy. Many other negative things filled the letter which she wrote to me.

I don't blame them for not liking you, I am afraid that I could not like you myself. This was my response to this dear precious young woman.

This was somewhat of a shock treatment, but the words that followed gave healing to her distraught spirit.

I said, "If you have no confidence in yourself, it is certain that others will tend to shy away from you."

I sent her scriptures to which I am about to introduce you and showed her how to confess favor and honor for herself with God and with others.

There was a dramatic change. Within a very short period of time she wrote back words of victory. "Brother Buess, it is working. I am, now, engaged."

Later, when visiting her city, she came to me and introduced me to her fiance, another one. Not too long after this she married the second lad.

Whether it is a teenage girl who feels frustrated, an adult man going for a job interview, or a wife seeking favor with her husband, these scriptures, properly applied, will change your situation. In many cases there will be a very dramatic change in a very few days.

Many have an attitude of insecurity within themselves. This affects their attitude toward themselves and also toward others.

Insecurity, fear, and frustrations of childhood may cause the individual to have the wrong attitude toward life and his or her place in it.

Ps. 8:5 "Thou hast . . . crowned him with glory and honor." Get all excited! God has crowned you with glory and honor!

Live expecting God's "honor system" to change your insecurity and frustration into success. God has crowned you with glory and honor.

> Jn. 17:22 reads, "The glory which thou gavest me I have given them . . ." You have the same glory that Jesus had. You truly have been crowned.

Imagine the Lord coming to you today and placing a crown of glory and honor upon your head.

You would live expecting things to happen. Doubt and insecurity would vanish.

Stand on God's Word. It is truth that sets you free. Faith comes by hearing the Word. Live expecting favor and honor to change your dissappointments into success.

As you believe that God has crowned you with glory and honor and favor, you will see success unfold before your very eyes.

> Jn. 12:26 "If any man serve me . . . him will my Father honour."

Most of you are truly serving the Lord.

You merely need to know how to apply the truths of the Word into daily success.

God has promised honor for you today. Past experiences and failures have conditioned your mind to accept disappointment and discouragement. Change your attitude, and let God be true and every man a liar. Let every experience be a lie. Bring every thought captive to Jesus. Make your thoughts line up with this Word. He is honoring you today. Expect miracles to unfold before you today. Favor and honor are changing your insecurity into success. Live excited!

Chapter 2

ABUNDANCE OF FAVOR
FLOWS FROM GOD
TO YOU

God has no limitations. You have no limitations except ignorance, unbelief, and flesh. Learn to renew your mind with God's spirit truth concerning favor with God and with man.

Change your negative confession of doubt and unbelief into a strong positive confession. God favors you. He loves you. There is a river of favor flowing to you.

Take a swim in this river of love and life, daily. You can watch tremendous transformations take place in your life, daily. You will, also, see great transformations take place in your associates. You will begin to bring forth good in others rather than evil.

Rom. 4:17 "God quickeneth the dead, and calleth those things which be not as though they were."

Words are spirit. Jesus said that His Words were spirit and life. Jn. 6:63.

These spirit words have authority over the natural world.

Speak these words on favor over and over during the day until your spirit is revived. Many people confess doubt and failure over and over during their lifetime until their spirit is depressed and broken.

A good strong positive confession of God's Word concerning favor with God and favor with man will put life into your spirit.

God Gives Abundance of Favor

Num. 6:25 "The Lord make his face to shine upon thee, and be gracious unto thee."

The Lord is in the business of blessing you. He makes His face to shine upon you. Drink in this truth. Breathe it deeply into your spirit. Bathe in the beauty of this thought. God favors you today.

Say it over and over right now. "God favors me today. God honors me today. I am a success today. I have God's special favor upon me today. He makes His face to shine upon me today. He is gracious to me today. I am someone very special with the Lord."

Imagine yourself in a large crowd of people. Suddenly, the spot light falls upon you. You are chosen for special honors. How great you feel that you have been chosen of all these people. A spirit of success and achievement comes into your spirit.

Now imagine yourself standing before the Lord. He calls you by name and says, "I am causing my face to shine upon you today. I am being gracious to you today. I am honoring you today."

How would you feel? You would get excited. You would leap for joy. You would lift up your head and get all excited about being alive in Jesus Christ.

You would feel success flowing from within. How happy you would be. You probably would not be able to walk for days; you would be flying.

Good news! God has already chosen you, called you out, and spoken these words to you. Now, stand forth and speak it to yourself until your spirit picks it up and comes alive in this great truth.

Filled With God's Fullness

Ep. 3:17-20 "That Christ may dwell in your hearts by faith; that ye, being rooted and grounded in love, may be able to comprehend with all saints what is the breadth, and length, and depth, and height; and to know the love of Christ which passeth knowledge, that ye might be filled with all the fullness of God. Now unto him that is able to do exceeding abundantly above all that we ask or think, according to his power that worketh in us."

Make a bold confession: "I am being filled with God's fullness. I am being rooted and grounded in love. God is doing exceeding abundantly above all that I ask or think. His mighty power is taking over in me."

Repeat this over and over. Do it several times a day. Your spirit will soon begin to respond to this medication.

Nothing Impossible With God

Luke 1:37 "For with God nothing shall be impossible."

Do not confess your negatives. Confess the accomplishment of that which appears to be impossible.

Confess that you are a success.

Confess that you like people and that they like you.

Confess that you are flowing in God's love, and that other people are being blessed through your life and ministry.

Confess that you are releasing God's miracle power, and that others are receiving healings, both in mind and body, through your words and ministry.

Nothing is impossible with God. He is in you waiting to be released through your positive faith.

Matt. 17:20 "If you have faith as a grain of mustard seed . . . nothing shall be impossible with you."

Get all excited!

God is in you!

His faith is in you!

His life is in you!

You can do things you never dreamed possible!

Begin to dream great things. Make larger plans. Meditate upon success in Jesus' name. Allow Jesus Christ to flow out through His Word of Faith. Encourage yourself today in success.

Expect the impossible to flow out through your life daily. Expect favor with people in every situation. Before leaving the house in the morning, speak words of faith to yourself and to your family or friends.

Expect to have nice situations during the day.

Turn bad situations into successes. Do not expect the negative. Have a positive attitude toward every situation. Jesus will soon flow freely through your life.

Zech. 12:10 "I will pour upon the house of David . . . the spirit of grace and supplications: . . ."

She was at school and the teacher said, "Virginia, what in the world has happened to you? You are beaming with love and joy."

"Oh," said the little girl, "The honey barrel fell over on me."

God pours out upon your house today the spirit of grace. Grace means favor you do not deserve. This young lady had been filled with the Holy Spirit. She had been baptized in God's love. Her definition of it was exactly right. God had dumped His honey bucket of love upon her.

"The truth makes you free," declared the Lord in Jn. 8:32. Speak this truth over and over. "God is pouring out upon me today the spirit of favor."

Do not accept failure and defeat. Lift up your head as if you were a king. You do reign in this life as a king, through Jesus Christ. Rom. 5:17.

Repeat this confession until doubt flees away. You have been blessed with God's grace. God has poured out upon you a river of favor with God and with those about you. Reject the things you have been feeding into your mind. Accept only what the Lord has told you.

He pours out upon you a river of favor.

Swim in it.

Enjoy it.

It is all for you today. Face life expecting something great to happen daily. It will.

Moody received such a divine flow of this river of grace and love that he had to cry out, "God, shut it off, I cannot stand anymore."

It is available for every one of God's children. May you be one of the many today who will tap into these divine resources.

Some men learn to walk in God's favor more easily than others. Let me introduce you to one preacher who learned to walk in the law of God's favor and success. When he went to churches to hold a series of meetings, he would have such favor and success that his meetings would last two and three months. Always, upon leaving such a church, the attendance would have doubled or tripled. The churches would continue in this success. This man was capable of passing his success on to others.

Later, he was called to a very small

country type church which was running under one hundred on Sunday morning. He called a church which was running five hundred on Sunday morning. He challenged this pastor saying, "In one year we will go around you in attendance."

The pastor of this larger church laughed at this; however, one year later he was not laughing. I was with the pastor of the smaller church when he checked the attendance of the two churches. His church had gone beyond the larger church by fifteen.

This man was acquainted with the operation of favor and success. He knew how to plan and think favor and success. He spoke favor. He lived in favor. He was a success. Why? With God, nothing is impossible. Let this truth take root in you, and you will never bring up the tail again.

This same man was called to appear before his boss while he was still employed in a plant.

"I heard you were using the empty building for preaching to the men," barked the angry president of the large company.

The reply, full of confidence and strength, flowed back in the affirmative. The president was so impressed that, before he knew what he was doing, he gave the man permission to use the building and ordered the company to buy song books, chairs, and a piano so the work could continue in a more definite way.

Expect to be kicked around, and there will be those who are eager to do it. Expect success and favor with God and man, and you will get exactly what you expect.

Lk. 2:40 "The child grew, and waxed strong in spirit, filled with wisdom: and the grace of God was upon him."

You can claim this favor, also. Jesus was human as well as divine. He was made like unto His brethren in all points. Read Heb. 2:17.

You are to follow his steps. 1 Pet. 2:21.

You are to duplicate His ministry. Jn. 14:12.

"The grace or favor of God was upon him." God's favor is upon you today. Live like it. Think like it. Expect good things to happen to you today. Do not leave the house without some spiritual exercise and prayer confessing this truth. Then confess it to the family. Get them to confess it together. You may have a friend whom you want to call to agree with you in this confession.

"My children have trouble in school, what shall I do? Their grades have dropped too low. Can you help me?" These were the words of a good neighbor.

I said, "Yes. Confess with the children daily the following. 'Jesus grew, and waxed strong in spirit, filled with wisdom: and the grace of God was upon Him'." Lk. 2:40.

She had them repeat this verse daily. After repeating the verse, they would then repeat it with their names saying, "We are growing in the Lord, we are waxing strong in spirit, and we are learning today. We have favor with God, with our school teacher, and with our fellow students."

Within a very few weeks both of her children improved his grades by two points. One went from F to C. The other went from D to B.

Insecurity and frustration had developed in the children's spirits. This affected their attitude toward life and their studies. When they fed truth into their spirits, success began to flow from them again.

The truth really does set you free.

Chapter 3

GOD BRINGS YOU INTO FAVOR WITH GOD AND MAN

Dan. 1:9 "Now God had brought Daniel into favor and tender love with the prince of the eunuchs."

Daniel was a captive. He was a foreigner. His people were hated in Babylon. There was no earthly reason for him to have favor with the leaders in this gentile court.

Why did he have favor? He had favor flowing from his spirit. He expected good things to happen. He had a healthy attitude toward others, regardless of his surroundings. He did not allow his adverse circumstances to turn him sour. He had a sense of success flowing from within. He knew deep inside that he was linked with the Lord. He had authority. He walked in strength and in victory. He may not have been fully conscious of this. It flowed out of him like a river. It was automatic.

He believed in the Lord. He and God made every situation come out in God's favor. He lived excited about life. Defeat and captivity of his people did not cause him to become discouraged. It challenged him to prove God under difficult circumstances.

Things in the natural looked bad, but Daniel knew that the spirit controls life. Rather than yield to his surroundings and become a failure, he arose to that level of victory into which every child of God should move. He determined to be a success by living in a spirit of favor and success.

As a result, Daniel became the prime minister of Babylon, the world power of his time. He remained in a position of leadership even during political upheaval and change most of his life.

"Your neighbor is angry with you about your dog. All of the dogs in the neighborhood are over there in his yard all day and all night. He is very angry with you."

This was the report that came to me long distance as I was out preaching the gospel of Jesus Christ. I had left my dog in the care of another neighbor.

"The neighbor who is keeping your dog is very upset about you and your dog," also, came the report.

This looked very bad to the natural eye. No one likes to have trouble with neighbors.

I spoke to my wife, and said, "Honey, I want you to agree with me. We have favor with both our neighbors. They love us. We love them. God is working this out."

This confession was continued from time to time during the next few weeks that we were out of town.

Upon arriving home, the first thing I did was apologize to my dear neighbor for the trouble my dog had caused him.

"Trouble you caused me!" exclaimed my neighbor.

"You haven't caused me one bit of trouble. It wasn't you, it was all of the other dogs that gave me fits. You had your dog tied; it was all of the neighbors who let their dogs run loose who made me angry."

This neighbor continued to be a very close friend. When I would leave town on preaching tours, he and his wife would cut our lawn, trim our bushes, etc., when they didn't like they way our regular yard man did it. This was especially true when they knew we were coming home.

Our other neighbor who had been in charge of our dog walked in our house and said, "Brother Buess, I'll have you know this, if you ever leave town again, I want you to give me the honor of keeping your dog. I love you."

Hallelujah! You get favor if you expect and show favor.

"Nobody likes us now. We have been filled with the Holy Spirit. Our church has relieved my husband from being departmental superintendent of the intermediates. I have been relieved from my teaching position in our church. Nobody likes us. It is so bad, when we walk down the street and pass one of our fellow church members, we know they are talking about us. What shall we do?"

"You have developed a persecution complex," was my reply.

Instead of expecting good things to happen, they were expecting bad things to happen, and they did.

I sent this couple the scriptures that I am showing you in this book. Seventy days later they answered the letter.

"We have confessed favor daily. We expect favor. We believe in success. We agree together before every committee meeting that we have favor. It is almost embarrassing. We seem to be like magnets. People seem drawn to us. We are like the hub of a wheel. Things seem to flow around us."

Hallelujah! They changed defeat into success by confessing and living God's Word.

Later, while visiting in this home, the husband explained a job opportunity which was available. He said that the very ones who had relieved him of his teaching position in the church were going to be the ones who had the say whether he got the job, or whether it went to another.

I encouraged him to apply the same principle of confessing favor and success. Several years have passed, now. This man has held this very important position in the community all of these years. He was placed in this position within a few weeks after our conversation.

His testimony at the time was, "The very ones who were against me, previously, came to me one by one and said, 'We are going to vote for you'."

God does bring us into favor with God and man.

"But I haven't held a job for ten years. I am a very poor typist. No one will want an older woman over a younger woman."

These were the words spoken to me by a middle aged woman recently. I encouraged her to confess favor and success with the job interview which she was to take a few days from then. This she did faithfully. She spoke success into her spirit. She began to live excited. Her spirit ignited with favor and success. Jesus and His Word were working in this child of His.

"Just as the Lord brought Daniel into favor and success he is also bringing me, Jane, into success," was her confession.

"What did you do to those men?" came the voice over the phone the afternoon of the interview for this job. "All they can do is talk about you. They have interviewed many girls all day long; but when they come out, they begin to talk about you instead of the girl interviewed. You have the job, Jane."

These were the words of a friend who worked in this office. Certainly, Jane received the job. She still has this job at the time of the writing of this book.

Later, Jane said, "Brother Bob, this job is a rat race. It is full of confusion. We are overworked. I don't think I can keep up with the demands made on me."

I said, "Jane, we are going to confess favor and success for you in this situation." Soon it happened. She was excited. The entire office was reorganized. New desks were placed in the office. She was somewhat perturbed when she found all of the other girls had a nice desk, but she had none.

The manager of the office came to her and said, "Jane, we have something very special for you." She was taken to another room. There was one nice big desk where she could be alone from all of the confusion of the outer office.

"We want you in here where it is quiet, and where you won't have to work so hard," was her manager's explanation.

She found herself with so little work to do that often she would relieve one of the other girls by doing some of her work. There was no earthly reason for her to have such favor.

You must remember that with God all things are possible. You must live in faith. Without faith you cannot please God. Read Heb. 11:6.

Live excited. Live expecting miracles to flow. The God in you makes you a success. Praise ye the Lord! Hallelujah!

Gen. 39:4-6 "Joseph found grace in his sight, and he served him: and he made him overseer over his house, and all that he has he put into his hand . . . the Lord blessed the Egyptian's house for Joseph's sake . . . and he left all that he had in Joseph's hand: and he knew not aught he had, save the bread which he did eat. And Joseph was a goodly person, and well favored."

Gen. 39:21-22 "The Lord was with

Joseph, and shewed him mercy, and gave him favor in the sight of the keeper of the prison. And the keeper of the prison committed to Joseph's hand all the prisoners that were in the prison; and whatsoever they did there he was the doer of it. The keeper of the prison looked not to anything that was under his hand; because the Lord was with him, and that which he did, the Lord made it to prosper."

Standing there being auctioned off as a slave certainly was no great inspiration or encouragement to young Joseph.

Listening to his brothers as they planned to murder him would have given the average young man a very rebellious spirit toward society and family, but this was not Joseph's response. He went about his daily duties with a spirit of success. He did not hang down his head in defeat and self-pity. There were no thoughts of despondency, or discouragement.

Life was a challenge to him. His victory was in the Lord and not his surroundings. He knew that through the Spirit of God he could change any surrounding.

When Jesus Christ and His truths are allowed to control the mind and spirit, you can change your destiny.

When the inner man is fed "Jesus food", all things are possible.

When the inner man is defeated and broken, you can only go backward and be tossed by every problem which the enemy throws your way.

Make your decision that you are the head and not the tail. Deut. 28:13.

You are in charge of every situation. You and the Lord tip the scales in your favor. Never look to the outward appearance. Always look to Jesus, the author and finisher of your faith. Heb. 12:2

Always expect good things to happen rather than bad. Bad things may come your way occassionally, but you can soon turn them to good.

If things seem to be going in reverse, just relax. Keep a constant attitude of success and favor flowing from God to you. Expect favor to flow to you even when it looks as if it is not. Extend favor and love to others. You must give favor to get favor.

You show mercy to obtain mercy.

You show love to have love flowing to and through you.

You give finances to release the financial flow in your direction.

You sow, and you reap what you sow.

Sow a healthy positive attitude about your situation.

Soon your situation will change. Your spirit will arise and take control of the situation. Remember; God quickeneth the dead and calleth things that be not as though they were, and they become. You are God's children. You are united to Jesus Christ. You, too, can speak things into being. Speak words of success. God will honor a good confession. He will always back His Word. Read Is. 55:11.

Looking to Jesus means that you stand on truths of the scripture and confess them instead of what you see around you.

This is like a missionary friend of mine who picked up a hitch hiker who was an escaped convict. He immediately pulled a gun on the missionary and threatented to kill him. This threw fear into the missionary at first. Soon he gained control of his thinking.

He told the man over and over that his gun was powerless over the situation. The missionary said, "I am a man of God. I have Jesus in me. Greater is He that is in me than he that is in the world. You have no power over me. I have power and authority over you."

This man continued to scream back at him "shut up." He continued to scream out, "I'm going to kill you."

The missionary continued to stand on the Word of God. He continued to speak his confession of faith. "Jesus Christ is in me. You have no authority over me. Greater is He that is in me than he that is in the world."

To make a long story short, the gun finally relaxed and dropped loosely in the seat. Soon the missionary prayed for the man, opened the door, put the man out, and went on his way to his wife and children in Mexico.

This is looking to Jesus and His Word rather than circumstances.

Favor flows when you stand on the living Word of God.

Favor flows when you stand on the Word of faith.

God's Word creates faith.

Circumstances do not always change.

Paul shouted himself out of jail one night. Later, he shouted for years and never did get out of jail; however, some of his greatest works were done right in jail.

One missionary fussed and argued with God because he was in jail. The Lord appeared to him and said, "I will never leave you nor forsake you." The missionary became very excited over this precious truth. It came alive to him. Jesus became so real to him there in jail that he was almost disappointed when he was released.

Learn to move in God's love and favor regardless of your circumstances. The circumstances may not change, but it is possible to move into a spiritual realm that makes the circumstances fade into the background.

The spiritual life and victory into which you enter are so real that they flood your soul. A higher life feeds to you from the spiritual world. Joy comes. Victory comes.

One missionary during World War II was a prisoner of war in Japan. The guards would kick and beat him. He was harassed. The missionary was constantly moving away from the gruesome realities into the holy presence of the Lord. He knew when the war was over before the guards knew. He lived in the presence of the Lord in extremely adverse circumstances.

You can create your own circumstances by entering into the presence of the Lord just as he did.

Many have said, "Even death is so glorious, I can't understand how anyone would hate to die." God's presence brings you into complete victory in every circumstance.

Now let us return to Joseph. He was in a bad situation in the natural, but it was in the plan of God for his life. God desired that he should be there so he could deliver the entire family from starvation. Joseph could have "blown" it all with a defeated spirit. He did not know for years why he was sold as a slave. He, later, saw the plan of the Lord.

As a slave he was so positive, alert, and successful in his speech and attitude that he was soon promoted. He was soon in charge of the entire house, money, etc.

"Joseph found grace in his sight, and he served him: and he made him overseer over his house, and all that he had he put into his hand." Upon studying this passage you will find that everything this Egyptian had was placed in Joseph's charge. The man knew nothing of his finances, etc. Joseph had it all. The man only knew the things that were on the table to eat. Joseph was in charge of the house. The wife even liked Joseph. She preferred him to her husband. Joseph refused to be unfaithful to his master. Remember that rule. Joseph served his master.

You must give if you expect a return. You sow good things. You soon reap good things.

Joseph was thrown into prison at the insistence of the enraged wife because Joseph would not commit a sex sin with her. She framed him. She lied about him.

He was soon demoted into jail.

Poor old Joseph. First his brothers tried to kill him. Then they decided to sell him as a slave. Then he was sold again in the market place. Poor thing, he must be "beat" by now.

Oh, no! "Rejoice in the Lord always" was his philosophy. "Praise God, here I am in jail," must have been his attitude.

"I am a success right here in jail," he kept telling himself. Everything looked bad. If he had thought on the past, he could have made himself despondent. He kept his thoughts on victory.

Soon, the jailer saw success in this young man. It took him about two weeks to change his situation there in jail. Within weeks, he was running the jail.

"The Lord gave him favor in the sight of the keeper of the prison. The keeper of the prison committed to Joseph's hand all the prisoners. . . whatsoever they did there, he was the doer of it. The keeper of the prison looked not to anything that was under his hand . . ."

Give Joseph one hour with the king, and he is running the entire country.

There was no defeat or failure in this lad. Circumstances did not change his attitude. If adverse circumstances hit you, rejoice. These are just getting you to the place you need to be.

It is the valley of Achor (trouble) where the door of opportunity and hope opens to you. Read this story in Hosea. 2:14-15.

God drew the children who were not where they should have been in their spiritual walk. They were off of the path of holiness and righteousness. They were missing God's plan for their lives.

He drew them into the valley of trouble. It was there that they repented, prayed, and sought the Lord. God then turned this into a door of opportunity for them. It was here that their first love was restored. Israel would sing as in the days of her youth. It was here that success came. He would give them vineyards from this adverse experience.

Repent, and then rejoice your way through problems. Have a strong positive attitude. Expect favor. Expect miracles. Believe in miracles. With God all things are possible. Speak that to yourself today.

God brings you through the fire and through the water to a large and wealthy place.

Know what God says about things. Do not let problems control you. You can control your circumstances with an overcomer's attittude. Dan 11:32. "They that know their God shall be strong and shall do exploits."

Live expecting great things to happen. This is faith.

Know your Lord. Know His power. He can do everything. He is doing it through you today. He is not limited by your circumstances.

You may be handicapped. Praise God, let it work for you.

You may have a lower mental ability than some. Praise God; smart fellows do not always bring home the best pay.

It is the lame that take the prey. Is. 33:23.

It is the weak that become strong. Is. 40:29

It is the worm with no backbone which God turns into a bulldozer with spiritual teeth which tear into any problem and cause it to dissolve. Is. 41:14-15

It is the foolish whom God uses to confound the wise. 1 Cor. 1:27

Your success and favor is not dependent upon being intelligent, ignorant, strong, or weak, but it is dependent upon knowing absolutely that your victory is in Jesus Christ and not youself. You know Jesus Christ through His Word.

You bring every thought into captivity to Jesus Christ. 2 Cor. 10:5 Your thoughts may want to run wild with doubt and fear. Make them come back to the scriptures on favor and success. Confess good things are happening to you today. Get all excited in His Word. Things will begin to change for you right away.

You are married to God's Son. You are in the family of God. Read Ep. 2:19 "You are of the household of God." You have a lot of pull with the "Top One." He is the Lord of Lords. He is the King of Kings. You are His favorite son. Live it up. Act like it. Live to the fullest of your inheritance. You are a joint heir with Jesus Christ. Rom. 8:17.

All things are yours. I Cor. 3:21.

> *Esther 2:15 "Esther obtained favor in the sight of all them that looked upon her."*

> *Esther 2:17 "The king loved Esther above all the women, and she obtained grace and favor in his sight more than all the virgins; so that he set the royal crown upon her head, and made her queen instead of Vashti."*

Esther walked before the king and others, and their hearts would miss several beats. She obtained favor in the sight of all who looked upon her.

Esther was an alien in the king's court. She was a Jew. The Jews were under severe attack at this time. Many were soon to die unless God intervened. Esther could have been very depressed and defeated.

Rather than submit to this attack of the enemy, she rose above the pressures and attempted to do the impossible. She released a spirit of victory and favor which caused the king to put the royal crown upon her head, and she became the queen.

Still the planned persecution for her people continued. Her life might soon be taken along with other Jews. Still she refused to listen to the enemy who was placing the circumstances and thoughts against her. She rose above her problems. She confessed favor with the king. The king granted her favor and blessings. Her people were saved. The enemy of the Jews was destroyed.

People all around you need help. Your family needs help. You are their deliverer through Jesus Christ. Get your eyes away from your abilities. Put them on God's abilities. Live as if you were a believer. Come forth into your strength today.

Confess: "Esther obtained favor in the sight of all who looked upon her. I shall have favor today with people. I will meet nice people today. I shall have good relationships with people today. I shall favor and honor others today."

Keep this attitude going all day. Expect to meet nice situations. You can actually draw the good out of bad situations with this faith and victory and favor spirit working in and for you.

Remove all of the negative attitudes toward others from your thinking.

You are learning to move in the law of success and favor. This is the beginning of a real love life in God.

You are now moving into the realm of complete transformation in your relationship with others.

Chapter 4

FAVOR WILL CHANGE HOMES, HUSBANDS, WIVES, AND CHILDREN

"Hello, Honey, look what I have for you," came the sheepish voice of her husband.

As the precious wife received from her husband a large expensive box of candy filled with his love and devotion, the wife vibrated with deep waves of excitement knowing what the Lord had done in the heart of both of them.

The following week the same husband marched home with a large package which contained a beautiful new coat which the wife had been desiring for some time.

This husband was not always so generous nor so thoughtful toward his little wife. His change of attitude came about only after his wife and children confessed, daily, for two weeks straight that they had favor with daddy, and daddy had favor with them.

They began to live expecting life to respond in daddy. Faith was working in their lives. God is not limited in any situation. God began to work things out. Miracles began to happen in this home.

You may have a situation on the job with your supervisor or with your employees. Apply this attitude of favor. Expect to meet exciting personalities alive with favor for you. Give them a break. You favor and honor them even if they, at first, knife you.

One woman was cut deeply by a bitter tongue in her supervisor. This supervisor had been giving her trouble for months. She was at the point of quitting the job due to the extremely bad situation between them.

One morning this lady had been confessing favor with her supervisor. The first thing the supervisor did was to knife her deeply with cutting and nasty words. Immediately the dear lady began to favor the supervisor with love and kindness. She said, "Oh, forgive me if I have offended you."

Her heart nearly broke with love and compassion for her supervisor. Within minutes this supervisor was saying to her, "Darling, can I do anything for you? Please forgive me for being so irritable." This was the beginning of a beautiful relationship. Goodness began to flow out of this supervisor.

Draw the good from people rather than evil. You are responsible to guide people rather than gig them.

Chapter 5

DRAW NEAR TO GOD FOR FAVOR THE ROAD TO SUCCESS

Prov. 11:27 "He that diligently seeketh good procureth favor: but he that seeketh mischief, it shall come unto him."

In Hosea 5:4 the scripture says, "They will not frame their doings to turn unto their God: for the spirit of whoredoms is in the midst of them . . ."

They would not frame or plan to do good. They were geared to the negative. They were geared to the self life. If anything offended them, they were on the defensive. They carried their feelings on their shoulders. They were full of vengeance. Hate was written on their faces. The following verse says, "The pride of Israel doth testify to his face . . ."

They were so negative and evil that it showed up in their faces. They were hard and harsh.

This spirit must be broken in your life. Diligently seek good from life. Expect good things to happen. They will surely come to pass. The scripture in Proverbs 11:27 teaches you to diligently seek and do good things.

You must put your heart into being good. To the individual who does this, favor will flow. "He that diligently seeketh good receives favor."

On the other side, if you diligently seek mischief, it will surely come. Constantly thinking problems creates more problems. Expecting to have problems causes you to gear every thought and pattern of your life to the attitude of problems and trouble.

You have Jesus Christ in you if you are a believer. You have an obligation to draw the good from situations. All things work out for good to those who love the Lord.

Matt. 6:33 "Seek first the kingdom of God, and his righteousness; and all these things shall be added unto you."

Draw near unto the Lord.

Let your love and devotion be first and above all else unto the Lord.

Seek His righteousness.

Develop the spirit of love for the Lord and for others.

Minister unto the Lord by being kind to both the lovely and the unlovely. Make it your mission to be loving and tender to others.

Take Jesus with you out into life when you leave the church.

1 Jn. 4:20 "If a man say, I love God, and hateth his brother, he is a liar: for he that loveth not his brother whom he hath seen, how can he love God whom he hath not seen?"

Live to be a blessing to others.

If you do not love others, you really do not love God.

Treat others as though they were Jesus Christ.

Determine to be kind to your fellow man.

Think of the kindness that you are going to give today.

You are now preparing the foundation of your day's activities. Expect things to happen today which never before have happened. Live by giving love. Live by giving a kind word. You are now moving into favor—the road to success.

Confess: "Today I will be a blessing to the Lord. I will be a blessing to others."

Chapter 6

GOD'S NATURE IS TO FAVOR OTHERS

You are made in God's image. The ability to favor others and receive favor is in you through Jesus Christ.

You are an heir of God through Jesus Christ. Gal. 4:7

You are a joint-heir with Jesus Christ. Rom. 8:17

You have God's ability within you through Jesus Christ. 2 Cor 3:5-6

You are a worker together with Christ. 2 Cor. 6:1

You and Jesus are joined for redemptive reasons. Ep. 2:5-6

God's plan is for you to go forth in God's ability and power, and favor others just as the Lord favors others.

Ps. 86:15 "But thou, O Lord, art a

God full of compassion, and gracious, long-suffering, and plenteous in mercy and truth."

Ps. 103:8 "The Lord is merciful and gracious, slow to anger, and plenteous in mercy."

Just as God is a God of love, He is also a God of favor. He seeks to favor and honor you today. A strong negative spirit will destroy your ability to reach out and receive much of this favor.

Constantly confessing the negative will keep God's love from coming through to you. It is like a road block or a short in an electrical circuit.

God is reaching out His hand to favor you. You must stop thinking that it can not be done. You must stop thinking that you are not capable of receiving or giving God's favor. You must stop thinking that you are not worthy of His favor. The Lord is merciful. He is gracious. He is plenteous in His mercy even though you may not deserve it. Come alive to the riches of His mercy and favor.

Now release this same love and mercy and long suffering to others. You are God's outlet for His love and mercy and favor to others. God's love and mercy flow through you. You are His ambassador. You are His co-worker. You are joined to Jesus for redemptive purposes. Come alive to your responsibilities and opportunities of being heirs of God and joint-heirs with Jesus Christ.

Gal. 6:7 ". . . Whatsoever a man soweth, that shall he also reap."

When facing new situations, look for the possibility rather that the impossibility. Look for a miracle rather than defeat. Go beyond anything you have done in the past.

You must plan your present situation. Reach out beyond your present achievements. Get out of the "rut" by planning and expecting to go to new levels of favor and success. Dream big. Thoughts are the beginning of great achievements.

Pr. 23:7 "As he thinketh in his heart, so is he . ."

The thing that you think on and meditate on will soon be in your front yard.

God favors others. You constantly meditate on blessing others. When you sow good thoughts to others, then you minister good actions to them.

The scripture teaches you to give, and then the Lord will make men give unto you. Give good thoughts and actions, and they will in turn honor you. The Lord said, "Be merciful to obtain mercy."

God is a God of love, favor, and mercy.

You must follow His steps. Gear yourself, and set yourself to be long-suffering and kind to others. Set yourself to be a blessing today. Exciting things are going to happen to you.

God is a God of favor, and He is constantly promoting those who learn to live in this law of favor. You draw on this favor in two ways. First, you expect favor to flow from God to you and from others to you. Second, you favor others even when they may not be so kind to you.

God is merciful to the unmerciful. He is kind to the ugly. He is long-suffering with His enemies. Develop this attitude of praying for your enemy. Watch your life leap into a new exciting role and experience.

Every situation will not turn out just as you want it. You must learn to flow with the attitude and mind of the Lord. You will have some situations which do not work out perfectly at first, and maybe some that never fully seem to work out as you expect. There will be plenty of situations, daily, that will reward your efforts.

We have already mentioned Joseph. He went through hell from time to time, but he always applied the law of favor. He found new excitements in favor with each new situation. He stayed full of expectancy. He refused to let circumstances control him. Each case of defeat was a source of challenge to him. He rose above his problems. The God of favor came through for him.

A THING TO REMEMBER

Is. 40:31 "They that wait upon the Lord shall renew their strength; they shall mount up with wings as eagles; they shall run, and not be weary; and they shall walk, and not faint."

Keep in mind there is a waiting for your ministry. God is a God of patience. John called it a kingdom of patience.

Do not allow impatience to destroy your road to success through favor.

> *"Wait on the Lord: Be of good courage, and he shall strengthen thine heart." Ps. 27:14*

Wait though He tarries.

> *Ps. 69:3 "I am weary of my crying: my throat is dried: mine eyes fail while I wait for my God."*

The psalmist, later in the same passage just quoted, said, "Lord, some of my problem has been my fault, but one thing I know, that those who wait on you will never be ashamed. I know you will come through for me." (5-6 Par.)

Chapter 7

SPECIAL FAVOR AND SUCCESS FOR THOSE WHO REALLY LOVE THE LORD

Ep. 6:24 "Grace (favor) be with all those that love our Lord Jesus Christ in sincerity."

God is a God of mercy and grace and long suffering. He blesses every person in a general way. He sends blessings upon the just and upon the unjust.

There is a special favor for those who really love Jesus.

This is the Peter, James, and John relationship.

Peter, James, and John were always the ones who received the mount of transfiguration experiences. John was always next to Jesus' breast receiving great truths and love.

Draw near to God, and you, too, can be recipients of His special favors. Jesus said,

"If any man serve me, him will my Father honor." Jn. 12:26b.

There is special favor above and beyond the general favor from the Lord unto those who move into that inner circle group.

God is honoring you, today, with success and favor as you receive this into your spirit. It will be necessary for you to release this love and favor to others for it to be fully effective. The dead sea is dead because it has no outlet. You become dead when you do not release God's blessings unto others.

GOD MINISTERS SEED TO THE MAN THAT IS BUSY SOWING

2 Cor. 9:10 "He ministereth seed to the sower."

As you give it out, God continues to fill your life with fresh love and blessings.

Electricity has no power until the circuit is completed.

Love and favor have no power until your circuit is completed. You must let it flow on to others.

PROMOTIONS FOR THOSE WHO LOVE THE LORD

Prov. 8:17-18 "I love them that love me; and those that seek me early shall find me. Riches and honor are with me . . ."

Riches and honor flow to the individual who dares to put Jesus first in his or her life.

Success lies at your door ready to be of service to you.

Faith releases the power of God. Success does not come from merely going to church and being a fairly good moral fellow. Success comes when one stands on truth. Truth sets one free.

Josh. 1:8 ". . . observe to do according to all that is written therein: for then thou shalt make thy way prosperous, and then thou shalt have good success."

One of the fundamentals of the law of the old and new testaments is to love God and to love thy neighbor.

Practice walking in love and meditating God's Word into your heart, and you will soon be moving in success.

Ps. 1:2 "His delight is in the law of the

Lord; and in his law doth he meditate day and night."

This man becomes strong like a tree planted by the waters. He bringeth forth fruit in his season. Whatsoever this man doeth, he prospereth.

As you love the Lord through His Word, a new fresh flow of success begins to flow through you. Continue to practice this meditation on the Word. You are loving God when you meditate on His Word. Release this love to the Lord and to others, and success cannot by-pass you anymore.

Live believing that all things are possible with God.

Live expecting riches and honor to flow to you from many sources.

Expect promotions to come.

Expect impossible projects to come into existence.

Expect God to give you answers to the needs of humanity that He has never given before.

This is the greatest day to be alive. Resources lie at your hands to go forth and do exploits. Invent that which is needed to bring about fuel saving automobiles, houses, office buildings, etc.

Let God make you a success. Believe for the impossible for you, today. The only limitation that God has is your lack of understanding of His laws.

Riches from God are at your disposal.

1 Cor. 3:21 "All things are yours."

Do not glory in others. All things are at your disposal. You have talents you do not realize. If you really want God to become angry with you, fail to develop the talents He has given you.

Mt. 25:28-30 "Take therefore the talent from him, and give it unto him which hath ten talents. For unto every one that hath shall be given, and he shall have abundance: but from him that hath not shall be taken away even that which he hath. And cast ye the unprofitable servant into outer darkness: there shall be weeping and gnashing of teeth."

The Lord was angry with this man for hiding his talent in fear and failure. Be willing to make a mistake. Dare to do something for the Lord. Do not stand idly by praying and asking God to do things that you must do in faith. You move forward by faith. Read 2 Cor. 5:7 "We walk by faith . . ."

God gives to the man that uses his talents, and he gets an abundance.

God takes from the man who will not use his blessings and gives to the one who uses his blessing.

I have noticed this in my life, too. I like to give to a successful person. I feel that he will use it to a good cause. A man who is small in his own mind is a poor investment.

God expects you to take what is at your hand and develop it. Many folks expect God to move for them. Faith says, "God has moved; now it is my move."

Moses prayed, "God, move; get this show on the road."

God said, "You get the show on the road." (Par. Ex. 14:15) "Wherefore criest thou unto me? . . . Lift up thy rod, and stretch out thine hand over the sea, and divide it . . ."

Often you cry out to God when God is waiting for you to move mountains by faith.

Speak to your situation. God can do anything through you. Your faith has to release before God can move.

Nu. 20:8 " . . . Speak ye unto the rock before their eyes; and it shall give forth his water . . ."

"Look out there and see our lovely new church building," said the pastor. The natural eyes of the great congregation could see nothing, but their spiritual eyes, trained to see the impossible, could see that lovely international center church edifice sitting out there with flags of many countries flying over it.

At this very time all natural resources had been exhausted to raise money for that lovely building. There was no hope from the finance companies or the banks for this large amount of money.

John Osteen continued to have his congregation speak to the rock of natural limitations that stopped the construction of that building.

"I spoke to that rock of limitations," cried Brother John Osteen.

His people continued confessing and speaking with him.

The convention was underway. The building was not the major issue at present. They were concerned in the work of God at hand.

At that very moment God interrupted the service. One man arose and pledged a large offering for the new building. Another arose and made another offering. Then a river of love flooded the congregation. Everywhere people were jumping up pledging offerings toward this building. After the money was counted they had several thousand dollars.

They started the building by faith. They depleted their account on several occasions, but God always brought it in as they needed it. They paid cash for the entire building as they built it.

You, too, can speak to your rock of limitations.

Expect good things to start flowing to you. Success comes as you confess, speak, and believe.

Never look to man for your resources. Expect God to move on men, but never get your eyes on particular men. Men will fail you, but God will never fail you.

As you go for a job interview, expect favor, but believe and look to God for it. This particular job may not materialize. Keep looking to God. He will never disappoint you.

Judges 5:31 "Let them that love him be as the sun when he goeth forth in his might."

Most of you love the Lord. Where is your success? You have not fully realized that God wants to bless you; so you go around in your negative world of fears, doubts, failures, and maybe someday I'll make it.

You have blocked your faith.

Go forth, today, singing, "I love the Lord. God is blessing me. He honors me today. I am strong like the sun in full strength. I am strong like the Son in full power. God is with me. I am His honored son."

Worship the Lord in this attitude. Live excited. Live expecting.

Chapter 8

SPECIAL FAVOR AND SUCCESS FOR THOSE WHO SEEK THE LORD

Jer. 33:3 "Call unto me, and I will answer thee, and shew thee great and mighty things, which thou knowest not."

Make a positive confession, daily, that you are a person of prayer. Keep this confession going. You may not be praying as you desire, but keep speaking it. Soon the positive will gain strength. You will find yourself flowing in the victory that your faith has created and spoken into existence.

You must become a man who walks hand in hand with God in fellowship, love, devotion, and prayer if you expect to succeed through His law of favor—the road to success.

There is no short cut. You must walk in holiness.

Negative confessions, that you are not a man of prayer, or that you never find time to read God's Word, merely create more defeat; and you continue to put off prayer and Bible study.

The more I confess by faith that I am a man of prayer, the more I find myself flowing in that vein. It is exciting to see God's law of favor and success bringing me into a fuller life in Christ daily.

Ps. 34:10 ". . . They that seek the Lord shall not want any good thing."

In Judges 18:10 the children of Israel were urged to go into the land of promise. It was a place where there was no want of anything that is in the earth.

You are in that spiritual land of promise today through Jesus Christ and the fullness of His Spirit.

All things are yours.

You are His sons.

You are His kings.

You are His priests today.

Satan is under your feet.

Failure is under your feet.

Poverty is under your feet.

Come alive, today. You are in the land of prosperity. Take it by faith. Live with this knowledge.

God has brought you to a place of prosperity in Jesus Christ. You can do all things through Jesus Christ. Phil. 4:13.

You are living in the land of no want. The Lord is your shepherd, and you need nothing.

God is the God of the supernatural. All things are possible with God. You are in His business. He is working through you. He is doing the impossible through you today. Live expecting the impossible to begin to happen in your life.

Too long you have sown the negative. You have anticipated failure in many areas of your life. You have expected problems in many areas. Your faith has been a dream rather than an actual experience.

Develop the attitude of, "I can do all things through Jesus Christ." Phil. 4:13.

He has blessed you with all spiritual blessings in Christ Jesus. Ep. 1:3.

You are complete in Christ Jesus. Col. 2:10.

You are sharing the life of Christ. You are sharing His ministry. You share His miracles. You share His possibilities. Hallelujah! Come out of your shell of fear and insecurity.

God brought Daniel into favor with the princes about him.

Confess: "God is bringing me into favor and success today."

A friend of mine heard me minister on favor. He came alive. He began to confess favor and success. His ministry began to reach our into new areas. Different companies and ministries began to deal with him and look to him for his services. This opened an entirely new out look on his ministry.

His own confession is: "I will confess success and favor until Jesus calls me home." Praise ye the Lord!

If you will expect favor to flow to you from your Father's table, then you can come and dine today.

Living in doubt, fear, frustration, and I

cannot do it will only bring evil into your life.

> Prov. 14:11". . . The tabernacle of the upright shall flourish."

This is God's promise to you. He has said that your house will flourish. Live in prosperity today. Believe for favor from life today. Give others honor and favor.

> Ps. 84:11 "The Lord God is a sun and shield: the Lord will give grace and glory: no good thing will he withold from them that walk uprightly."

Jesus is your shield from failure.

He is your protector.

He will not withold good things from you today.

> Ps. 92:12 "The righteous shall flourish like the palm tree: he shall grow like a cedar in Lebanon."

It is God's plan to prosper you. It is Satan's plan to get you to accept failure. You must make your decision to follow the Lord's plan for you.

The enemy wants to make you sick, sad, and fearful. He desires to destroy you. Jn.

10:10 "The thief cometh not, but to steal, and to kill, and to destroy: I am come that they might have life, and that they might have it more abundantly."

Refuse the negative. Refuse the failure. Arise into life abundant provided by Jesus Christ.

Rebel against the failure spirit that Satan has tricked you into accepting for your life.

God says you will flourish. Identify with this truth. It is the truth that sets you free. Do not look at your surroundings. Do not look at your present or past achievements. Look unto Jesus. Look unto this truth. "The righteous shall flourish." Stand on this. Make every thought become a captive of Jesus Christ. Make each thought agree with this truth. You shall flourish like a palm tree.

A palm tree is a rugged tree. It can be mistreated; it will still grow. Its surroundings may be negative, but it reaches its arms to heaven and its roots deep into the earth and draws from hidden resources contained therein.

I saw a group of palm trees growing in a rock canyon in Arizona. There was nothing but desert all around, but here stood this grove of palm trees. People passing through had burned some of them, but they still grew. Others had been bruised badly, but they still grew. There was no surface water, but their roots ran deep into the earth reaching hidden waters.

Your church situation may not be perfect, but you can take hold of Jesus and draw from His power. You can root into the Word and flourish like these palm trees. You can be persecuted and actually thrive on it. Your family situation may be sour, but you can still come into success. Your success is not dependent upon your surroundings, but it is dependent upon your attitude and understanding of your ability to reach into Jesus Christ and live in His strength.

Chapter 9

CONFESS FAVOR

CONFESS FAVOR WITH YOUR FAMILY

If there is a problem in the home with any member, sit back and relax. Get in control of the situation. Believe that God is smiling upon you and your life. Confess that your children love you, and that you love your children. Confess that your husband loves you, and you love your husband. Confess that your wife loves you, and you love your wife.

Refuse to accept the negative in these areas. Refuse anything you see on the surface that would tend to discourage you. Take charge of the situation by believing for favor and success in your family.

CONFESS FAVOR WHEN COMING INTO A NEW SITUATION

As my wife and I come into new situations, new cities, or new churches, we always confess favor with the people. We agree together that God will give us favor with the people, and that we will show love and favor to them.

It is exciting to see the Lord begin to change lives and cause people to see our ministry through the eyes of love.

We consider this a foundation stone in our ministry and success.

As you come into new situations, live in excitement. Live expecting good things to come. This is putting your faith into action.

CONFESS FAVOR WHEN TRAVELING IN FOREIGN COUNTRIES

Situations can be serious at border inspections. Seek the will of the Holy Spirit. Do only what a perfect God would have you do. Expect great things to happen even in a tight place. God can get you through places quickly. He can give you favor with the officers in charge, and great things will happen to you.

Missionaries can especially cash in on this as they are traveling and moving from one situation to another. Many times they are in hostile areas. As they believe for favor, they will be surprised to see God perform miracles above and beyond the normal.

Many times God gives favor to you when you do not know how to confess favor and success. How much more will He do it when you know the law of God's favor.

One missionary was trying to get something across a check point at the border, and they would not let him pass. He went to the next entry point. They still stopped him. At the next entry point he discovered that they were calling ahead. They greeted him as follows, "Well, we have been expecting you."

He began to confess favor and success just before arriving. He got out of his vehicle and told them exactly what he had in his truck. Then he said, "If you fellows don't stop hindering the gospel of Jesus Christ, God will punish you. I am bringing this equipment here to help your country and your people. I plan to go through this gate with your permission."

They called the offical in charge over them, and he granted the missionary special permission to pass into the country.

Many missionaries could tell you hair raising stories of their success and favor in situations like this.

One friend of mine was taking the Bible into a closed country. He carried one Bible in his hand. He had Bibles sewn in his overcoat. The guard at the gate asked him if he had any more of the books like he had in his hand. He told them that he most certainly did. The guard motioned him on through the gate. We do not know what the Holy Spirit made the guard hear, but we do know that God gave him favor.

CONFESS FAVOR WITH BUSINESS ASSOCIATIONS

Many times things become serious between men in a company. Go forth with victory; God is changing everything around. You will be so excited when you come home after a day of favor and success in situations that normally would have been defeat.

CONFESS FAVOR WITH MEN WHO HAVE DISAGREEABLE PERSONALITIES

Some men and women get up on the wrong side of the bed on some days. Others get up on the wrong side of the bed every day.

You can sit back and see serious situations change in the lives of others as well as yourself.

Project a love spirit

Business meetings sometimes become very tight and edgy.

A man of success will be sensitive to the Holy Spirit. He will seek wisdom and confess favor. He will confess that God will put words in his mouth.

One man moved into a sour situation where men and wemen were being very unthoughtful of each other. The meeting was cold and icy. Before entering he confessed favor and success. He believed that they were responding favorably to the Christ Spirit in which he walked. Within minutes after he entered, the entire meeting changed to a light, happy meeting.

You get what you believe.

Est. 2:15 ". . . Esther obtained favour in the sight of all them that looked upon her."

Imagine yourself as being like Esther. Her greatest beauty came from her pleasant spirit, not her outward appearance. Feel yourself flowing in favor with those about you. As you do this, you will automatically begin to respond by giving others a smile and a healthy respect. You will automatically begin to honor those about you.

Chapter 10

DO NOT ACCEPT THE PAST AS A RULE FOR FUTURE LIVING

You can stay in the same old rut and be very little different until you go to be with Jesus, or you can enlarge your ministry.

Is. 54:1-3 "Sing, O barren, thou that didst not bear; break forth into singing, cry aloud, thou that didst not travail with child: for more are the children of the desolate than the children of the married wife, saith the Lord. Enlarge the place of thy tent, and let them stretch forth the curtains of thine habitations: spare not, lengthen thy cords, and strengthen thy stakes; for thou shalt break forth on the right hand and on the left . . ."

You can do this. You are supposed to do this. You are to sing your way to victory. Confess victory and favor before it becomes a reality.

Enlarge your ministry and outreach by faith. Soon, you will see the favor begin to work. It is very important to sense the will of the Spirit of God for your life. Spend time in prayer concerning new outreaches. Confess favor and guidance in each situation. Then, slowly begin to step forward into new areas; it may be purchasing new land; it may be building new buildings; it may be enlarging your business; or it may be entering into new ministries such as soul winning, radio and television ministry, etc.

Do not move out too quickly. Test the Spirit for guidance and approval as you move out. Be willing to withdraw certain steps and move in other directions at the guidance of the Spirit.

Someone said, "I do not want to get in the flesh and fail God."

You had better get in the flesh and fail than sit there and rot not trying to succeed. You will be in the spirit more times than you had thought.

Let success live in your spirit. When you exercise the fundamentals of faith, then God begins to do what you formerly considered impossible. Make yourself available to receive favor and honor.

Jesus said, "If a man serve me, him will my father honor." Jn. 12:26

WRITE DOWN ON A PIECE OF PAPER THINGS THAT YOU DESIRE TO ACCOMPLISH THROUGH FAVOR— THE ROAD TO SUCCESS.

Make a list of places in which you need favor during the immediate future. Then make one which deals with the visions you have in your spirit for victories in the more distant future.

Look at the past and decide to improve upon your situation. Expect God to help you move out of your rut through favor— the road to success.

I always have a confession that deals with distant future things in my ministry. Remember; there is growing envolved in favor. 2 Peter 3:18 "Grow in grace, and in the knowledge of our Lord and Savior Jesus Christ."

Confess that your ministry is maturing.

Confess that your life is taking on new responsibilities.

Make a list of those things which you desire to come to pass in your life. Some will take weeks and months. Others will come to pass almost immediately.

When you have reached certain goals, then move out for greater goals. Never allow yourself to reach the point of "having arrived." Discouragement and disillusionment will set in rapidly if you do.

One man, whom I recently counseled, was at the point of physical sickness due to retirement without a plan. He was so sick and confused that he found it difficult to get our of bed in the morning. If he had had a program in mind upon retirement he would have moved into a new challenge which would have driven him forward and lengthened his life.

Success comes as you push forward in favor. You are to go from one glory to a new glory. 2 Cor. 3:18.

BRING YOUR DREAM INTO REALITY

After you have prayed and confessed favor in a new situation, then put it into action. Step out, and do the thing you never did in the past. This may be to start a new prayer group or a new ministry outreach. It may be starting a new branch business or adding new departments within your present business.

Try not to get yourself out so far that you cannot get back to land if you find yourself moving in the wrong pattern.

KEEP YOURSELF IN BALANCE

There is a thin line between the will of God and the will of the flesh. Make a bold confession that you are moving in His will and that He is guiding you.

Jn. 16:13 "When He, the Spirit of truth, is come, He will guide you into all truth . . ."

God is guiding you. Expect this favor. Confess this guidance. He is guiding you today.

Refuse the negative confession of, "Poor old me. He never guides me." This is destructive to favor and guidance. Get yourself into the victory line with a healthy, positive approach to your situation.

Do not move out without prayer, sound advice, and serious thought. Faith does not always follow human advice. Train yourself to know when God is leading you beyond the natural. Keep in balance to the best of your ability.

Refuse to move out on fleshly impulses.

Keep yourself completely surrendered to Jesus Christ.

May your constant desire be only God's will for your life.

Learn to recoginize the ego of self which wants to gain esteem. Your desire to be a success is to bring glory to the Lord Jesus Christ.

Chapter 11

SPECIAL TESTIMONIES ON FAVOR

A Teenage Girl Receives Job

A young woman stood in one of our services in Alexandria, Louisiana, and gave a glowing report.

She said, "Brother Buess, I want to give testimony on what favor did for me after hearing you preach the Word of God on favor a few months back. I went in for a job interview. I was too young. I was only going to be there three months, and the employer wanted a permanent employee. I had confessed favor on the way for the interview. I had confessed favor the day before with regards to this interview."

"The man read my application and then turned to me and said, 'Why do you think I should hire you?' "

"I am a blessing everywhere I go," was

her response. "I am a blessing to my employer," she continued.

The employer responded, "I thought I had a girl hired for this job before you came along, but now I am not certain."

"I need a full time, permanent girl," said the employer. I can't understand why I am hiring you knowing that you are leaving in three months."

She stayed with this man for the three months. He was well pleased with her. As she was making final plans for departure from the office at the close of the tenure of her employment, the employer said to her, "Can you find me someone else who is full of life and victory such as yourself? I have never had such a pleasant experience with any employee."

Missionary Finds Favor With Business Men

Recently a friend of mine found favor in very important operations of his missionary enterprises.

After hearing this message on favor, he began diligently to apply this truth. He compared it to a river of favor everywhere he turned. Different ones began to contact him to help him promote the work of the Lord.

A Banker Finds a Powerful Tool for Operating a Bank

Recently where I had been ministering, a banker approached me. He began to tell me what a blessing the message on favor had been to him.

As I listened, he told me that he keeps the book *Favor, the Road to Success* in the bank to give away to his employees and customers.

He was excited. He said, "I go to work excited. I anticipate the law of God's favor working in our bank. It is like going to church. I expect favor to flow in the office with the employees and with our customers."

Recently he made a visit to one of the other banks with which he was affiliated. He said, "I was shocked into reality. It was like a rat race." It was some time before he had visited another bank after he had learned the law of favor. This bank knew nothing of the law of favor. Confusion reigned. He said, "Man, was I glad to get back to peace and favor with God and with my associates."

I was in a southern state recently when I was approached by another banker. He had about the same testimony about favor with God and with man. He had given one of the books *Favor, the Road to Success* to a customer. This man was having some serious financial trouble. The customer was so excited that he placed the book under his pillow and slept on it. He was excited about God's word on favor and honor both with God and with man.

The banker brought this customer to church with him that day to meet me. The customer had a testimony that he wanted to share with me on the results of God's favor in his life.

He said, "After I placed God's word under my pillow, a miraculous thing happened to me. A man came up to me and gave me an outright gift of several thousand dollars. My crisis was met. I was able to get out of the financial pressure I was under."

By the way this book on favor has many scriptures from the Bible. This is what the man was referring to when he placed this book under his pillow. It was not that he considered this book on favor as the Bible. He was excited about God's word in it.

A Father Shares His Testimony of How His Son Found Favor at School

I was in west Texas. A brother in Christ came into the meeting just as the service was about to begin. He approached me and said, "Sometime I would like to give you a testimony about how my son found favor to be a great blessing in his life."

I told him to give it to me real fast right then.

He said, "My son was failing every subject when he was passed to the 9th grade in high school. About that time he was handed a copy of your book on favor. He read it and was fascinated. He read it again several times. He began to claim favor with God and man. He claimed favor with the teachers and fellow students. He confessed that as Jesus increased in wisdom, he too would increase in wisdom."

The testimony continued. "My son has just recently graduated from high school. He confessed favor for four years. It worked. He was on the A honor roll. This meant that he had to be on the honor roll every time during his last four years in school."

Praise the Lord for people like this finding favor with themselves and those about them.

As you develop confidence in yourself, your whole world changes. Your outlook changes. The real you can come alive and manifest itself. The Lord Jesus can come forth and manifest His personality and His mental ability in you.

700 Club Believes in Claiming Favor

Pat Robertson has given away thousands of these books on favor to the people who watch the 700 Club. He has given it to all of his employees. Everywhere we go we run into people who received this message from the 700 Club as a gift.

Continuous Flow of Testimony on Favor

I have had people stand in line three and four at a time to tell me how this message on favor has changed their lives. One girl said, "This book saved me." Another girl standing by said, "Me too. I was just about washed out when I received this message on favor, and God helped me to get it all together again."

Favor on the Job

I have had many, many, many people testify to a complete about face in attitudes on the job. They were getting stomped and trampled before application of favor truths. Then things began to change. They were treated with respect and honor.

Honor is in you. Believe in the Jesus of honor, and He will flow through you. When your attitude changes, people change.

You Need to Keep Going Over These Scriptures

One man came to me and said, "I thank you for reminding me to get in favor again." He said, "I really had this working but I gradually began to taper off, and it is not working as well as before."

Rom. 1:7 ". . . Grace be to you and peace from God our Father, and the Lord Jesus Christ."

Grace is favor you do not deserve or merit.

Grace or favor is like a brake on the

automobile. It is there for you to use. Use it and enjoy it.

Favor works in every believer to a measure, but once you begin to stir it up, it will work in many more areas.

I Never Dreamed I Could Apply This in That Area

Many people have come to me with problems. When I tell them to confess favor, they look at me in amazement. "Oh, I never dreamed of applying favor in this situation."

I personally have found that you move into favor by levels. You learn to confess it in one area and forget it in another. So keep at it. It keeps unfolding into greater dimensions.

The Testimony of Ruth and Favor

Ruth 2:2 "And Ruth the Moabitess said unto Naomi, Let me now go to the field, and glean ears of corn after him in whose sight I shall find grace. And she said unto her, Go, my daughter."

Ruth was a gentile. She was now living in Israel. This made her the underdog. She was certainly of the minority race.

Take a look at her spirit. "Let me go to the field . . . I shall find grace (favor)." She had a very positive attitude about life. She was sure she would be successful. She confessed favor before she left the house.

How did her confession turn out? There was no doubt about it. God was working. Her confession of faith in herself and in God being with her was paying off well.

Ruth 2:3-9 "And she went, and came, and gleaned in the field after the reapers: and her hap was to light on a part of the field belonging unto Boaz, who was of the kindred of Elimelech. And, behold, Boaz came from Bethlehem, and said unto the reapers, The Lord be with you. And they answered him, the Lord bless thee. Then said Boaz unto his servant that was set over the reapers, Whose damsel is this? And the servant that was set over the reapers answered and said, It is the Moabitish damsel that came back with Naomi out of the country of Moab: And she said, I pray you, let me glean and gather after the reapers among the sheaves: so she came, and hath continued even from the morning until now, that she tarried a little in the house. Then said Boaz unto Ruth, Hearest thou not, my daughter? Go not to glean in another field, neither go from hence, but abide here fast by my maidens:. . . I have charged the young men, that they shall not touch thee? and when thou art athirst, go unto the vessels, and drink of that which the young men have drawn."

Normally a gentile would not be received with such kindness, but this was a person of a different nature. She believed in favor instead of racial problems or rejection. The workers of Boaz recognized something in her and gave her permission to work in the field with the other maidens.

When Boaz arrived from Bethlehem, the first thing he said after he greeted his men was, "Whose damsel is this?"

It must have been love at first sight. Her strong spirit of favor disarmed this great man. The first thing he did was to order the men to leave her alone and let her drink of their water and eat of their food. "And Boaz said unto her, At mealtime come thou hither, and eat of the bread, and dip thy morsel in the vinegar . . ." Ruth 2:14.

Then after this he ordered his men to drop some barley on purpose and let her actually glean among the sheaves. ". . . Let her glean even among the sheaves, and reproach her not: And let fall also some of the handfuls of purpose for her . . . rebuke her not" Ruth 2:15-16.

Ruth had so much favor with Boaz that she actually proposed to him. After they were married, Ruth gave birth to Obed, who became the father of Jesse, who became the father of David. So Ruth, the gentile woman, had so much favor with God that He overlooked His law forbidding the marriage of an Israelite with any other people, and she became part of the lineage which brought the Messiah, Jesus Christ, to the world. Praise ye the Lord!

I Never Dreamed I Could Have This Nice a Job

One lady stopped me before church one day and said, "I have read your message on favor. I began to apply it. I now have the best job that I have ever had in my life. Before I read this message I never would have had confidence to apply for this job. The Word on favor built up my confidence. I just made application for a job that yesterday I would not have dreamed possible for me. I know I have that job and I am thrilled with Jesus."

I rejoiced with her. Hallelujah!

A Salesman Rejoices in Favor

"They told me never to come back. I did go back. They said, 'We do not like your product or your company, do not come back.' Then I read your message on *Favor, the Road to Success.*"

I stood in front of that business, confessed favor, and went back again. Now it is one of the best customers I have. They turned completely around when I changed my attitude about God's favor and my own confidence in God working in me."

This is one of many similar testimonies that I receive often.

I Have No Job, What Shall I Do?

The pastor encouraged the man who had just recently become a part of their fellowship. Then the pastor said, "By the way, let me share a book with you which has been a blessing to many in our fellowship."

John took the book and was instantly captivated. He read it and reread it. He confessed the scriptures on favor. Later he made application for a job about which he knew nothing. They hired him and sent him to school for special training. He was with the company less than a year when I met him. His take-home pay for one week was more than the average person makes in one year.

Needless to say John gives these books away by the bundles.

By the way, John is a fictitious name, but the story is true.

A Pastor's Testimony on Favor

"I have been teaching from your book on favor for a year now. It has turned our church around. Our people are blessed. Would you please come and share with us on favor?"

I went. I was blessed. The people were blessed.

My Own Testimony

"You really do not have to bother with this."

"Oh, yes, let me see if this won't work

out better." He kept fumbling through sets of schedules.

"You really do not need to bother about this."

"Oh, no bother, let me see something else, it may work out in this way." He kept going through more books.

"Please do not bother, it will be all right just as it is now."

"Oh, no, just a minute, I believe I have it."

I had asked this man if it were possible to do a particular thing. To tell you the truth I have forgotten what it was I was trying to do. It could have been a change in a schedule on a plane or something of a similar nature. His response was emphatically in the negative.

I then thanked him and was about to leave when he began to contradict everything that he had previously said. The thing he said could not happen happened even while I insisted that he forget it and he kept insisting that he believed it would happen. Praise God for His favor.

A Negative Report on Favor

"I do not believe in favor. It does not work." "Why not?" I responded.

"I confessed favor for a certain job, and I did not get it. It does not work."

"It is not supposed to work in every situation. God is sovereign. He knows what will work out right in each situation. If you had favor in every situation, you may get the wrong job, the wrong mate, or the wrong whatever."

Do not give up. If favor does not work in each situation, do not throw up your hands in disgust. Keep pressing forward. Usually things begin to happen right away. Other things take more time. Some things are not supposed to happen. Hang loose and re-joice always regardless.

Paul's Testimony of Favor or Grace

I Cor. 15:10 "But by the grace of God I am what I am: and his grace which was bestowed upon me was not in vain . . . "

"It is not me. It is the grace and favor of God which makes me what I am," said Paul. God's favor changed Paul. His favor was given to Paul, and he responded by walking in it.

Favor is like a train. You choose to get on the train and cooperate with the train. If you do not jump off of the train, it will carry you where you are going.

Do not jump in and out of favor. Hang in there by faith and it will bring you through.

Remember, you stay on your train by faith. Favor or grace is poured out on you just as it was on Paul, and it will take you to great heights in the Lord.

Paul tells us that God's favor took him from being a murderer to being a soul winner.

Col. 1:6 "Which is come unto you, as in all the world; and bringeth forth fruit, as it doth also in you, since the day ye heard of it, and knew the grace of God in truth."

"It has been working all over the world. It has been bringing forth tremendous changes in lives. Heathen are being changed. Fruits abound everywhere. I also expect the same to happen to you."

This was Paul's confession about grace or favor. It has brought forth fruit everywhere it goes.

Walk in favor, dear one.

You too will have grace — fruit in which to rejoice.

Favor is a choice. You can choose life and success by choosing to walk in favor. Or you can choose to be a bum and, with very little effort, you soon will accomplish your mission.

Choose to be a winner. When the men and women set out to win in the Olympics, they pay a price. They work at it daily.

You have to put forth effort to keep favor flowing.

Tit. 3:7 "That being justified by his grace, we should be made heirs according to the hope of eternal life."

It is by his favor and grace that you have been made an heir with Jesus is Paul's testimony.

It is like a set of twins. One is pulling the other along and saying, "Come on. We can do it. Just step out in grace, and we can do it together."

Jesus has made you an heir with Him by His favor. Learn to submit to His guidance. He will lead you forward. Expect favor to bring you into the full ministry of Jesus.